EXCERPTS

I Shed my Shield in final surrender and
open my Impassioned Heart;
This Cloistered Soul
now breathes New Life;
This Key, this Gift
has made it so.

Shall we seek to see the Truth
and make peace with the universe?
Come to me now Theópnuestos,
"Breathe into me" the Truth.

Perhaps it is the human frailty
of being bound by all things measured.
Seconds ticking...hours wasting;
Days gone by and how much life is left to live.
The speed of light in time and space,
an effort vain and futile.
Let us rather watch a plant grow,
hold an ancient hand and feel its history;
Feel the Sun and breathe once more.
Breathe Life Eternal into your Soul
for it is Now and it is Here

To be made naked of all once held so dear...
and if this punishment is all that comes
from past transgressions,
my gratefulness is profound,
for a darker place well could have been.

ENTHÉOS
"GOD WITHIN"

INTIMATE REFLECTIONS FOR THE INTROSPECTIVE

by *Vincent*

A Compendium Series by
Light of Mind

A Compendium Series
Copyright 2015 by Luzimen Group Inc., Publisher
www.lightofmind.us

Design by Jenny J Taylor
Illustrations by Jeanine Christman Handell

All rights reserved under the Pan American and International Copyright Conventions

No part of this book may be reproduced in whole or in part, scanned, photocopied, distributed or recorded in any manner whether printed or in electronic format now existing or hereafter developed without the express written permission of the publisher except for brief quotations or excerpts from critical articles and reviews.

ISBN: 978-0-9968594-0-0

For my mother, Luciana, a Bearer of Light.

LYCEUM: A PLACE OF LEARNING

I have been asked by several friends why I wrote these personal reflections and why I write at all. It occurred to me that these writings are a personal and natural flowing of multiple concepts and ideas that have come to me over a period of time. As I write, I have a profound sense of sharing the immense spiritual gifts I have received. I had a spiritual metamorphosis at the age of 14 after I had served a funeral Mass as an altar boy and was on my way back to school. I volunteered to serve these funeral Masses often. It was unknown to me at the time as to its intensity and the impact it would have on my life, but somehow, I knew something substantive had changed in me. I was never the same. I believe it was a combination of my Mother's strong and peaceful spirit and the observation and internalization of the mourning and grieving of those who had lost a loved one. I believe that their spirits gave me this gift. It is a gift of Peace and Strength that is a challenge to explain because they are so profound and personal.

Everything changed. I was spiritually undefeatable. Yet it was years before I understood what had transpired in me and to me, and until I understood its Power.

I am aware that most people never experience something so profound, especially at such a young age, if ever. Having been given this gift, if there is sin, it would be sin not to at least attempt to share this with others. It is a responsibility to open minds to different levels and kinds of thoughts to create freedom of the mind. It is not easy. It is important to me to touch one mind. It could be you. Transforming my spirit driven thoughts into words is the easy part. It is the understanding of the words that is difficult. My writings are not easy to read and interpret and may require multiple readings and study.

A close friend asked me "why don't you write your poems and other writings in a more simple form so that more people can understand and accept the message?" My response to her was that I write what the spirit channels through me, hidden messages and multiple meanings included. This means that many of the concepts and energies in my writings require thought, study and discussion, even if alone with your own thoughts.

My goal is to share the ideas of open and honest thought, discussion and inquiry. The pursuit of truth, whatever it may be and wherever it may lead, **without fear of reprisal.** We should be prepared to question those "certitudes" that are held as fact, and we must inquire about anything and everything that is pursued with Purity of Intent. My son Joshua once told me that the greatest gift I gave him was that I taught him the concept of thinking. Thinking sounds simple enough but it is much more than simple thoughts we have every day. It is the discipline of inquiry about ideas which we have been conditioned to accept as fact or faith and listening to the discussion that occurs in your mind.

It is interesting how religion puts "God in a box," and how people accept these temporal and physical notions of God, promoted by humans. How can something so immense and incomprehensible be described in the frailty of feeble words? The dichotomy for me is that I must use feeble words to try and express the essence of God.

The great philosophers in history simply asked questions or perhaps asked simple questions. They knew there may not have been an answer, but they asked questions about life, meaning, purpose and God, knowing that the questions were perhaps more important than the answers, because they knew there were no easy answers.

In the end, this is an inquiry about self and your ideas and relationship with God. This is a discussion about what you think. This is a platform for seeking truth.

ACKNOWLEDGMENTS

I would like to acknowledge...

Jenny J Taylor (jennyjtaylor.com) for her counsel and assistance in the design of this book.

Jeanine Christman Handell (jeaninechristman.com) for her insightful contributions to the kinship of writing and art as you will see manifested in her illustrations.

Albert Handell (alberthandell.com) for his heartfelt and soulful Foreword.

Dodici Azpadu, MFA, PhD, novelist, short story writer, poet, sage and Professor of English at the University of New Mexico for her instructive, discerning and nourishing commentary.

FOREWORD

It gives me pleasure to write this Foreword for *Enthéos*, created by Vincent.

Upon meeting him I immediately felt something special. Was it his quiet pleasant manner, his warm smile and easy-going gaze or was it simply his handshake...? He came to our house to meet my wife Jeanine, who is the illustrator of this book.

As we sat and he spoke, I immediately realized I was not with an ordinary soul.

Then he read the Poem "GATHASPA" (My Father). The opening sentence did it for me: **"I don't remember the day or moment I set eyes upon him."** I was immediately an infant like him. That went deep within me. He continued the reading, which brought tears to his eyes. What a beautiful personal way of presenting a newly-born child becoming aware of his dear father.

From birth he becomes a young child: **"Total devotion became the sibling of abject dependence."**

As Vincent's relationship with his father beautifully develops into maturity and more **"The enigma was in the knowing in my soul that his love was tethered to a past of withered expectations."**

One reads further: **"He did know my devotion and *Enthéos*. Thus, he paved the boundless path to the dialogue of learning."**

When the reading and the absorption of the reading subsided, he spoke casually of being in prison and what a wonderful experience it was. Vincent is not a violent man or common criminal. He was incarcerated for 2 years because of a business misdeed for which he accepts full responsibility. The incarceration was a blessing in disguise. He had the time and the environment to focus in on and finish this beautiful work... this tome of personal reflections.

His thoughts are rich, insightful and autobiographic. His message and his reading of his writings brought to mind an old proverb that I always relished "One can forget what one has spoken, but one does not forget how one felt."

Albert Handell
www.alberthandell.com

"True freedom is of the Mind and Soul;
No shackle can bind you and keys will not set you free."

TABLE OF CONTENTS

Page	
1	**Prologue**
5	**I Enthéos -** The Great One is not "out there." God is very near.
17	**II I Fagio -** Nature sends us messages and sets us free to fly.
23	**III Numinous -** Can we ever comprehend the mystery of creation?
29	**IV Theópnuestos -** God breathes Oneness into all things.
37	**V Veritas -** Truth? It simply "is." Look beyond the veil.
43	**VI Sentience -** To know that we exist is the "God Key."
49	**VII A Breath of Adonai -** Feeling God. Trandscendence.
57	**VIII Seattle Woman -** Learning the Language of Listening.
63	**IX Memento Mori -** Four spirits are created and make a grandson.
69	**X Perdition -** How much is enough? Just a little bit more.
77	**XI Cunundrum -** We don't have things. Things have us.
85	**XII Embrace -** Learn to see God in all things.
91	**XIII Vitam Aeternam -** Life eternal...it is now.
99	**XIV Liberatus -** Redemption and reconciliation free this man.
105	**XV Repentance -** I ignored God's great gifts and now pray for a new banquet.
111	**XVI Lapsit ex Caelis -** It fell from the heavens, this gift.
117	**XVII Luminous -** Are you listening to your Messenger?
123	**XVIII Gratia Plena -** Being full of Grace and Gratitude.
129	**XIX Enclave -** How does it feel to walk to the gates of freedom?
135	**XX Gathaspa -** My Father. A telling of the Brotherhood of Surrender.
143	**Final Thoughts**
145	**About the Author**
146	**About the Illustrator**
147	**About Papyrus**
149	**I Am**

PROLOGUE

The thoughts in this book were prepared for the "deep thinker" that resides inside of you that you may have yet to discover. These personal reflections and introspections are a chronicle of a personal journey and story of meaningful parts of my life. They are expressions of both everyday events and soulful revelations as they unfolded before my eyes and spirit. For example, *Veritas* is based on a spiritual experience I had with a Filipino fellow inmate while I was in prison; *Seattle Woman* is about a woman I saw on a bus in Seattle that touched my soul in a meaningful and unusual way, though I never spoke to her; *Memento Mori* talks about a friend I consoled because he had lost his grandmother while he was incarcerated and felt helpless. I wanted to write a poetic history of how he himself came to be and how he couldn't help but love his grandmother; *Enclave* discusses my approaching departure from the prison; *Gathaspa* is a recounting of my relationship with my father and *I Fagio* tells the story of a glorious community of yellow breasted black birds that made the prison their home for a few weeks out of the year and the messages I received from them.

While there may seem to be religious tones in some of these writings, the intent is not to wax religious, but instead to explore the self and the spirit within the self. Unfortunately, most people who need nourishment of the spirit, do not find God within, but seek to be "fed" their faith by others, whether by individuals or organizations. This ignores the absolute Power that already resides within oneself and relinquishes that Power to others. This is akin to "filtering the faith" and partaking only of that which others interpret for you instead of having a true and direct relationship and discovery with God.

I wish to share my experiences and thoughts in the form of intimate writings, short stories and narratives. As with most things, there are multiple interpretations of the written word. What comes forth from the mind of each person is a reflection of their perspective and personal journey. Take your time to read, absorb and understand the messages in these personal writings. As you read and study these messages and as you write your own comments, thoughts, questions and personal revelations, this book will come alive for you as you consider thinking original ideas and questioning old ones. Consider this a journey of inquiry; a quest for "sophos," wisdom in Greek. Perhaps it can be a mindful and thought provoking investigation of the world and universe in which we live.

What is Truth?

What is right and what is wrong? Why is it right or wrong?

Why is something right today that was wrong yesterday?

Why am I asking these questions and thinking these thoughts?

Where do these thoughts originate?

Will my thoughts live on after I die physically?

Do I make free will decisions or are things determined?

Do we really know what God is?

Is God its own creation?

Our thoughts should be provocative. There is another world that exists that is wholly different from the conventional world and the so called conventional wisdom that permeates everyday thinking of the majority of people. We exist in mental prisons that in many ways are far worse than cells and chains. I challenge you to challenge conventional thought; to have original thoughts that you may be fearful of thinking because they don't follow so called accepted and "settled" facts. Today, we need heuristic thinkers; *those who possess or develop the ability to discover and learn things for themselves.* Albert Einstein engaged in a process called the "thought experiment" where he imagined himself as an integral part of the problem he was attempting to resolve. This led him eventually to the development of his theory of Special Relativity, a groundbreaking advancement in scientific thought. Because we are so conditioned to accept and respond to society's norms, we are also conditioned to "not think" about things we may question deep inside. Why? Because we are comfortable with the status quo which we hope lasts a little longer and we don't want to create discord; because when we think and act outside of tradition we can then become ostracized and accused of heresy, treason, betrayal or apostacy as the case might be. Human nature desires acceptance, not exclusion and ridicule. We all want to be included. Hitler said, "how fortunate for governments that the people they administer don't think." He relied on that credo to dominate millions of unthinking and devoted believers. Independent thought can be a lonely raft in a vast ocean. Yet nothing changes unless and until something or someone changes the way we think about things.

It seems that we have forgotten and ignored the deep and resounding messages from ancient minds whose enlightened thoughts apply as much today and perhaps even more than ever before. We are at the precipice of a New Age of Enlightenment. Never before has the world needed enlightened thought as much as it does today. It needs you.

You can be an integral part of that Universal process.

You have already begun...

ENTHÉOS

We all have a supernatural presence within us. I call it "Enthéos"; **God within.**

The etymology[1] is from the Greek "Theos," meaning the Mighty One. The word Theos itself has its origins in the name "Zeus." The word "*enthusiasm*" is derived from the Greek concept of Divine Inspiration. In Latin it is Deus. In Spanish, Dios and in Hebrew, the tetragrammaton,[2] YHWH (or Yahweh), Adonai, along with Elohim and El. There are many names for God. Every culture that believes in God has a name for God. To a great extent they are all names (or titles) that attempt to describe or identify the same Entity. Other beautiful names or references for God are:

Elah; Aramaic (Awesome, Fearful One)

Kami; Japanese (Divinity; Spirit; Mind)

Khuda; Urdu and Persian (Lord)

Tao; Chinese (The Way)

Shang Ti; Chinese (The Supreme Ancestor)

Al Ilah; Arabic (The God)

I Am; the Great Causation; Eternal Mind; Original Mind; Silent Intelligence; Essence of Mind; Timeless Witness; Infinite Consciousness; Heavenly Master; the Great Amen; Shaddai; Eternal Embrace and many others.

If you read closely, you will see similar names, titles and descriptions within these writings. They are wonderful references and names for an entity that defies description. Yet, within the limitation of human language, we attempt to define and describe that which is indefinable and indescribable. While reading and thinking about these writings, thoughts and narratives, look inside your soul and spirit…to find The Spirit within. The great thinkers in history did it. You can do it as well.

---

1 Origins; derivation of words and their meanings.
2 Consisting of four letters.

Carry this book with you and perhaps when you are feeling alone, fearful, desperate, angry or seeking enlightenment, you can read from these writings and find comfort, consolation, tolerance, hope and guidance as you include and write your own thoughts into it. You will find that you have Balance and Power living within you that no one can take from you. It is that singular essence that you **do** possess above all else, when all else seems to have descended to unimportance. It is the most simple of things, yet it is the most powerful force in the "Eterniverse."

I spent two years in a federal prison. I do not define my life based upon that experience, but it was meaningful and instructive. As I look back at that time and what I observed and learned, it was most impressive and enlightening to view people and the world, including the outside world, from such a perspective. The revelation of the meaning of people, friends, family, possessions and our desire to exert control over things were the most interesting. I experienced something that 99% of society will never experience. I consider it a gift from *Theos*. I found Clarity and true Liberation through imprisonment. Some of these writings and thoughts come from that perspective. Others are simply personal reflections and inquiry about existence and the universe…and why things are or are not.

True freedom is of the Mind and Soul; **No shackle can bind you and keys will not set you free.**

I
ENTHÉOS

*It is our nature to continue the pursuit of
Purpose and Meaning because it is that very pursuit
which gives Meaning and Purpose…*

ENTHÉOS
THE BEGINNING

At the beginning of time, when God created the Eterniverse and all of the many wondrous elements within it, the Creator also then set out to create Man and Woman. By then Lucifer was reigning in Hell, rather than serve in Heaven and was thus predisposed to challenging God in all things since his lot had been cast to rule in Hades and roam the Earth in an eternal search to create discord. He soon discovered through his many devious sleights of hand that the Great One was to create a very special being that would be like the angels but would dwell on Terra. Upon learning of this new Creation, Lucifer hastened to have conference with the Almighty to present a most interesting proposition to this Creator who had so powerfully and disdainfully set him down upon Gehenna with such finality that it gave rise to his infamous words in Milton's "Lost Paradise":

Said Lucifer,
"Hail, horrors! Hail infernal world! And thou profoundest hell,

RECEIVE THY NEW POSSESSOR…

One who brings a mind not to be changed by place or time. The mind is its own place, and in itself can make a heaven of hell, a hell of heaven. What matter where, if I still be the same… Here we may reign secure, and, in my choice, to reign is worth ambition, though in hell:

BETTER TO REIGN IN HELL THAN SERVE IN HEAVEN…"

With this bitterness turned to dominion, Lucifer, the former "Bearer of Light," from which his name derives, conspired to hide God from humans, that they would never know Enlightenment but dwell in servitude to all things physical and of the World. In his matrix and labyrinth of deception, he boldly and unabashedly challenged The Omnipotent in a manner that so ensorcelled[1] Him, that the perfidy[2] was lost in the challenge.

Lucifer said, "And what of this creature you would create and make a little less than the angels to spring forth from Your Mind,

---
1 Enchanted; fascinated
2 Deceit, betrayal; treachery

fully grown and pure of mind and soul?"

"And what know you of My Mind and of this new Being which is so dear to Me that I shall make him in My image?" challenged the Great One.

"You know," said the Adversary, "that You made us too, like You in mind and spirit, though we now be denizens of a different domain. Our lot is cast, this we know, but in Your Perfection, could You create another who would fall like us though Your design would contemplate that it could not be so? Surely Your new creation would be so perfect so as not to fall to such temptation that would, once succumbed to, deem himself again Your equal as did we."

To which God roared, "He will be both obedient and perfection and your wiles shall not his mind alter!"

"Then let him choose, and if he chooses darkness over The Light, then I shall be allowed to hide You from man," spake Lucifer.

"Your proposition is pure folly and so I will allow it. You may go about your foolish errand so that if your workings make him fail, you may attempt to hide him from Me. But the bargain is not complete," said the Almighty. "You may hide him where you wish and I know you will choose well, but if someday they come to find Me after being hidden deep, your chains on him shall be loosened forever more and you will be dead to him in his soul and in his spirit. I will thence reclaim him as my special saved creation."

Baal replied, "Very well then, let us set upon our work to see if what God hath wrought on Earth will bring paradise or pain."

And so Lucifer usurped the Garden and the two who dwelled there with the fruit from the Tree of the Knowledge of Good and Evil, as we know the story well, and as a part of his grand bargain now won, he schemed to hide God from man in a place so deep and so remote, and so far from man's reach and mind, that he would never find Him despite his every effort.

Thought Satan, "where shall I hide God that humans will never find Him? I shall hide God in the most distant, most remote forest, so filled with the fiercest, most fearful creatures that humans would never venture there!" he said with glee. Then thinking more he realized that this creature was far too clever and persistent, and somehow would find and enter this forest and there, find God hidden and the grand bargain would be lost!

Not yet in despair he conspired and thought once more. "Yes, I have it!" he announced to all his fallen brethren. "I will hide God in the recesses of the deepest and darkest canyon on Earth. Man can hardly scale such depths, much less go into that dark place where I shall hide their Creator." Then once again he pondered this and knew that this creation would someday probe these deep and distant depths as well and the contract would go against him.

The discouraged devil sat in despair glaring at the universe as he labored desperately to find that place so profoundly distant, man would never reach out to it. He considered the heavens, then altered his thoughts from the infinity of space to hiding God in the smallest of all things, the atom. "That too is a universe unto itself and humans will never know that they are a universe unto themselves as well." Yet he knew that humans would someday solve that riddle too, and once again the arrangement he had made with The Mighty One would destroy his pursuit of the domination of humans.

There seemed no answer to this monumental, nay, eternal question and so, at the moment of surrender he decided to dwell with man and learn his mind for only in this manner could he hope to resolve this maddening query. So he lived as one of them but none of them knew him or recognized him, and thus they shared with him all manner of hopes, fears, loves, agonies and those uncontrollable things called emotions. But above all he discovered that they had an emptiness in their eternal search for Meaning, for Purpose, for God, for their Creator. And so when he asked them where they would look for God they replied that they looked everywhere they could see; the forest, the desert, the deepest canyons and the heavens.

And when the Adversary heard this he knew then where he would hide God; where man would never think to look for God and therefore never find Him.

"Aah yes," he thought as it struck him like a light from the heavens, a gleam filling his eye. For he knew he had won the grand bargain.

"I will hide God within the mind and soul of man himself. He will never think to search for Him there."

It is the quintessential[3] quest of humanity to find meaning in our lives and purpose for our existence. It is as essential to our spiritual survival as are air and nourishment to our physical bodies. It is also very fascinating that we look for Meaning and Purpose in things outside of ourselves whether in possessions, reputation, fame, churches and even in people. We are constantly looking to explore that last frontier. At the beginning of the migration of the human race to all parts of the world, there was always that last frontier beyond what we could see that drove us forward and ever further, always needing to find what lay beyond the sunset and sunrise or beyond the next mountain range and deep canyon. Then we learned to move across the oceans whose expanses were far greater and more dangerous than on land, yet again, we looked and pushed further. Now we find ourselves peering through space and beginning to travel and understand its incalculable vastness searching for answers to the time and place of our origins. We are even starting to plant the seeds of exploring time, past and future. In all of that Herculean[4] effort, what exactly is it that we seek? The meaning of temporal life? The purpose of our existence? How it all began? Why we exist at all? Or the great ontological question: "**Why** is God?" Perhaps we seek answers to questions not yet posed. And perhaps the one question that may be the most difficult: what would you do if you found those answers? Would you be satisfied? Would you believe it? Would you finally be at Peace and search no further? Would

---

3 The most perfect or typical example of something; classic.
4 From Hercules; formidable; difficult; grueling; back breaking.

you need more "evidence"? What if that which you learned isn't at all what you expected? Or is it our nature to continue the pursuit of Purpose and Meaning **because it is that very pursuit which gives Meaning and Purpose?**

Because we are physical beings, we are driven by physical stimuli. We are chained by the physical world despite the fact that we claim so many freedoms. We are bound to a corporeal plane of time, space and things both physically and mentally.

But those who think deeply like some of the ancients, experience a revelation about the real Treasure that lies within that can make you unshakeable and undefeatable. It is not to say that it is a bad or evil thing to have a good life with all of the accoutrements such as a nice car, home, job, clothes, reputation, fame and even luxuries. Those can all be good things. After all, what is good and what is evil? Are drugs good or evil? Most people will say that they are evil because "they" cause so must damage in society. Of themselves, they are not intrinsically evil, just as other things in the world are not good or evil. They simply exist. They don't do anything of themselves. It is the attachment to them or misuse of them, including misguided beliefs, that creates discord in the world and obfuscates[5] the Ultimate Power from us. We seek it everywhere but within. And it is there in the Soul that we can find Enlightenment.

This is no easy path because it is not entirely in our nature to behave in this manner. Why "not entirely"? Because I believe that God created us to be like angels as well as human. And so we struggle with both the human and the Divine, and that is, I think, where our search for Meaning and Purpose derives. We know that we will be human until we pass, which is a very limited time. We also believe that after we pass, we will be spiritual in an existence that is not bound by time or space. That is the Essence that we struggle to know and understand while here in this temporal world. It is a great conundrum[6]. But there is a good and Sacred Path you can follow to find Balance and Power and it is within your reach.

---

5 To be unclear or confusing; to blur or cloud
6 A problem or difficult question; dilemma; a quandary

Stop…Breathe deeply. Take your time and slow down. Think profoundly. You will find Inspiration within. The word "inspire" derives from the Latin word "inspirare" which means to breathe in or to inflame. In the middle ages it meant "under the influence of God." It also means that Inspiration is the Creator's breath within;

Your **Enthéos**.

Seek to understand the Power within and break the chains of the supposed Grand Bargain that hides God from you. Your personal **Enthéos** awaits your inquiry.

Inspiration from "You are Power Filled" by Ordaris Jordan

II
I FAGIO

The Hearing in the Heart is for those Enlightened

I FAGIO
I FLY

My awakening today is Luminescent[1]
and the Energy is thick like fog;
the vision into their Collective Soul
is uplifted by their Celestial Harmony.
The anticipation overwhelms me.
I have witnessed their Heavenly Dance before,
but today, now, this morning is more Intimate.
For on this day, in this time, at this place,
I think I know what I shall see.
10,000 Sentinels Standing Strong against the wind;
No! Not wind! The Breath of Elohim under wing.
10,000 golden breasts bursting forth
against the Sun from arboreal perches.
And in each, beats their song
in soulful unison.
The Symphony is frenzy to a shallow spirit,
but the Hearing in the Heart
is for those Enlightened.
10,000 voices singing praises to on High
to a crescendo; one song,
a Reverent Rejoicing.
But what is their Purpose;
Their meaning here?
They live free within these prison walls,
immune to rules and cells and keys.
What shall we learn
from their Unchained Nobility?
The answer now takes flight.
Then these 10,000 Strands of Life
singing now with one Pure Voice
bring my contemplation back to the now.

---

1 Radiant; shining bright with light from within.

Their Sacred Utterance
rises to Primeval Shout
in Sacrosanct[2] Exuberance…
Then…in One Mind and Soul together,
SILENCE…
Now 10,000 golden jewels take flight at once.
One strong breath
lifts them all together.
Incomprehensible is a word unworthy
in description of their Eloquence.
These Ten Thousand are but
One Mind, One Body, One Spirit,
their aerial ballet, Honey Flowing from Heaven
like the Word and Reason of Shaddai,
The Almighty,
sweet to eyes so starved for Beauty.
And now upon being witness
to this Sacred Orchestra,
I come to know why they traveled here;
To free my own imprisoned Mind and Soul.
I shed the Chains of Servitude
and lift myself with them;
Now, Ten Thousand and One…

I FAGIO!! I FAGIO!!

I FLY!! I FLY!!

---

[2] Sacred; respected; hallowed

The World and Life send us messages incessantly. But we are mostly blind and deaf to these celestial messages. We can see and hear them if we learn to observe and listen for them. Perhaps we do see and hear them but are fearful of their meaning. Our antennae, our frequencies, are not tuned into these other dimensions that exist all around us because we are so immersed in the temporal world. In many ways we fear leaving the "comfort" of this world to really understand the voices in the mist of existence. Because we have a need for the security of what we think we know, we avoid or simply reject that the Eterniverse is talking to us in a different manner; in a different language. We must learn a new language of "listening."

Are you chained in a mental prison? Do you have room in your life, your mind and in your spirit to fill them with uncharted Meaning and Purpose? If you stop and listen and truly observe, this dimension will provide you with messages that can ascend your understanding and create apertures to another world of existence. First you must shed your fear and open your mind. Learn the language that doesn't rely on words. The language of the Soul. The language of Listening. Adjust the frequencies in your vision, hearing and in your Soul and soon you will have a new Universe to learn and enjoy that exists within you.

III
NUMINOUS

*This Universal Soul has keys solely for
the Great Transcendence.*

NUMINOUS
SUPERNATURAL, MYSTERIOUS, HOLY; IMPOSSIBLE TO DESCRIBE OR UNDERSTAND

It stands before me in Noble Grandeur
existing solely from rapture past;
There is no answer to the query
the whence and why of this new Essence.
The light of history shines through space eternal;
This eloquence of infinite celestial candles
arriving now through time and space as
we set eyes on that which is no longer.
A fragile but inquiring mind
born in the noble passion of this being
stretches far to capture meaning
of this Numinous Sacred Harmony.
But in this reverent inquiry
we find the pursuit eternal too,
for what appears to be but one
is countless members in that order.
We see, we count, we think we know,
but the abyss is most profound
and has its secrets chained and guarded
from relativity and quantum quotient.
No!!, This altar is not for knowing;
The search for Meaning is its Purpose.
This Universal Soul has keys
solely for the Great Transcendence.
And in this mystery exist yet others
for in the universe that is the corpus
live countless worlds like those above;
Living Strands of Being grand and small.
And as they dance so intimate

we witness their universal alchemy,[1]
as countless billions near and far
perform in vestigial[2] auditorium
peering through time and space immemorial.
Yet we ponder its conception;
"Who" and "what" and "how"? we ask,
and most important, "Why?"
The "Who" is the Great Causation,
Essence of Light and Eternal Mind,
although this is no answer
to those who live and seek in science;
"What", is simply what we see
or not see, for a riddle it surely be;
We measure space and time and size
In defiance of their nature.
The mind cannot conceive the "How"
for it is "Opus Dei," "the work of the Creator";
Failed attempts to replicate are
vindication of its prism.
Aah!! Comes now the eternal proposition;
The "Why" burns in our souls,
the purpose not to be revealed
for this, deciphered cannot be.
Now rest your Spirit, Soul and Mind,
surrender soulful to the Great Amen;
Numinous, Sacred Sacrament
embraced by Spirit and Peace of Deus.

---

1 The seemingly magical process of transformation or creation such as changing lead to gold.
2 Residual leftover remnant of something that was once much greater or larger.

The universe, or Eterniverse as I call it, has questions we cannot fully answer or comprehend. Its creation; its creator; why it was created, etc. Yet we have inumerable answers to so many questions posed over eons. The body of knowledge we have accumulated over thousands of years is almost inconceivable. We seem to know everything about everything. But it seems, the more answers we have, the more questions are bound to follow in a never ending cycle of not knowing. Our quest for knowledge and answers has taken us into a vortex from which there is no escape. Can we ever know everything? Do we want to know everything? Should we know everything? This is where Faith and Fact can both come together in confluence,[3] or separate in conflict. To some, Faith is a fact. To others, Fact has no relationship to Faith. Yet even those who count on fact only, have faith in that very belief, albeit based on empirical "evidence." I have never heard someone state that they "have fact in their conclusions," but I have heard people say that they have "faith in their conclusions," which seems a bit of a dichotomy.[4] Even those who relentlessly pursue scientific facts must be fueled by some sort of faith that they will "discover" the answer not yet revealed to them, or they wouldn't push to find it. Perhaps the answer is that we will only know everything when we are no longer bound by these temporal dimensions and even then, if that happens, will it matter?

---

3 The meeting or merging of two things such as two rivers (ex. the Tigris and Euphrates).
4 Conflict; contrast; difference

IV
THEÓPNUESTOS

Is it fear or is it courage that moves or makes us still? It's that which has most value to each within his circumstance.

THEÓPNUESTOS
PR. THEÓ-NOS-TOS
GOD BREATHED

I look at countless stars in the Firmament
and I see but One;
And as I pass through worlds so distant,
their pulse is singular, not many.
Our abject fears and highest hopes
come from the mind of Everyone;
The apogee and perigee
are measured 'gainst just one,
as must the equinox and solstice.
We know to love and learn to hate;
Two sides of well worn coins.
Is freedom free, or does it cost?
Imprisoned solely in the mind, Yes,
the talents due are mental walls,
not bars and keys and cells.
Friend and Foe are but the same
from one day to another,
for what's revealed is benefit
hidden in their shadows.
Is it morning, noon or night?
It matters naught, the time is now;
Like eternity itself
which knows no Alpha or Omega.
And what of birth
and what of death?
The spirit knows no difference;
Both are one to the Creator.
Detritus[1] fallen in Gehenna,
The Master's Touch does make a Treasure.
And who has wealth and who has not?

---

1 Debris, waste, rubbish of any kind

Are poverty and riches both imposters
feigning who its owner truly is?
In what dominion is it written
that homely is not pulchritude?[2]
Only in that one with corpus
that sees no deeper than the flesh.
What we think we see and know;
It's delusion,...not understanding.
The hubris of our judgment
fed by only one perspective.
And so it is for doubt and Faith,
it's hard to tell one from the other;
For each has within its soul
seeds and roots and borrowed branches.
And what of Light
and also darkness?
The one could not exist
but for the other being.
Was he honest or deceitful?
To her, Truth was but falsehood afoot
because the prism of perspective
yet again distorts the vision.
Is the Cross death or Life?
The symbol can perplex.
Dismas[3] *calls out to Life,*
while Gestas hears the voice of darkness.
This air we breathe, this oxygen,
was venom once for all that lived;
To Adam came, a Man of Clay,
new breath called Theópnuestos.
Is it fear or is it courage

---

2 Beauty
3 Dismas...Gestas: Dismas was the "good thief" and Gestas was the "bad thief" crucified with Jesus.

that moves or makes us still?
It's that which has most value
to each within his circumstance.
Who is master; who is slave?
For now it may be such;
But in that Revelation soon,
the slave may be the master.
The demented and the mastermind, are
two sides of a translucent page.
And so it goes ad infinitum,
these lenses that we see through;
Shall we seek to see the Truth
and make peace with the universe?
Come to me now Theópnuestos,
"Breathe into me" the Truth.

Perception. We live in a world where one thing, one event, even so called history is viewed from different perspectives. We seldom know the entire Truth about anything. Have you ever thought that much of history is not at all what we have been led to believe? We "know" for example that history is written by the victor. How much different would the histories of the Battles of Hastings or Thermopylae be, if written from the perspective of the vanquished? Even the chroniclers of the victors would have a different story when viewed from different vantage points. But so often politics, religion, hubris, fear, greed and vanity select the facts then color them as they never really occurred and are then painted in a tone favorable to those in power. This is true with politics, religion, love, war and virtually every human endeavor for which we have so called recorded history.
Some people even make up history by repeating their story so often, it becomes accepted as fact. Then it gets printed a few times and suddenly it becomes a "reliable source" or an "accepted fact," and henceforth everyone believes it to be truth when it isn't truth at all.

Many times it is difficult to distinguish between fact and fiction, strength and weakness and other seeming opposites. For instance, a person's greatest strength can also be their greatest weakness. Someone asked me once how her cats that had such quick reflexes and are so attuned to their surroundings could be caught by a coyote. I waited until a cat was stalking a rabbit in the yard. I pointed out how the cat's greatest strength was its total concentration and singular focus on its prey to the exclusion of everything else, otherwise it would miss the opportunity to spring at the exact right second. At that moment is when the cat is most vulnerable to an attack by a coyote watching from behind, because the coyote has a distinct advantage while the cat is oblivious to its presence. It's all about your point of view, your perception of things. Interestingly, Montaigne noted, "When I play with my cat, who knows if I am not a pastime to her more than she is to me?"

When I was in prison, I remember thinking how some prison guards and employees seemed to be in a far worse prison than

I was. It seemed most of them disliked their jobs and were unhappy. It certainly made one wonder why they remained, but they were captives of a system that gave them what they believed to be security, benefits and for some, the important position of empowerment. Now, having left there and having paid my debt, I am free and some are still there paying theirs. In a very real way my mind was always liberated and they were prisoners of their positions.

We carry these pre-conceived notions or conventional wisdom with us. What exactly are "conventional wisdoms"? They are conditioned responses based on what we believe to be truth and facts. Indeed, why do we consider someone ugly versus someone who is ostensibly beautiful? What is Up and what is Down? It depends on how you are conditioned and where you are. That really smart person who is a genius is many times so near to what we believe is insanity. But is it? The history of the human race is replete with judgments about Right and Wrong. And over the centuries we have made Right into Wrong and Wrong into Right and we have wars, politics, religion and borders to prove it. The dichotomies are endless.

Think about things and seek the Truth. The Truth is unbiased. The Truth does not have a country, political party or religious persuasion. It simply exists without any support or detraction from us, nor does it need us in order to exist. If God is Truth, would It not want you to find It?

V
VERITAS

He is me and I am He, the Great "I Am" ennobled us.

VERITAS
TRUTH

I held his hand and felt his pain;
the pain transcended that of most,
and then as if about to feign
I saw the Spirit was his host.
His eyes were tired, yes, but shining;
Looking, seeing past the rapture.
Truth…his soul it was divining;
Sublime peace he yearned to capture.
And as he shed his isolation
God's countenance did he portray;
So eloquent a conversation
that every fear He did allay.
And now my hand receives his blessing
flowing through me unabated;
Soul now open and confessing
cannot now be separated.
He is me and I am He,
the Great "I Am" ennobled us;
This new Domain has set us free
and breathes new life in Veritas.

Have you ever spent time or known someone who was, or seemed to be holy? Someone who felt like they had a mystical or divine presence about them? It is a most impressive experience. I have had the good blessing of having met and known such people. One of those is my mother, Luciana. Another was this man I met while in prison. To look in their peaceful and powerful eyes and to hold their hand and literally feel their peaceful power flow into one's body is transcendent. But one must have a "listening" for it and more importantly, you must allow it to happen without fear. Yes, without fear. Most people are fearful of opening their hearts and souls to others. This is something you can experience with a person you have never met before. We go about our days distracted by the world and we ignore the preciousness in other people and therefore we miss seeing and feeling who they really are. Make a note of this and see if you can connect with someone in this manner. You will not believe the sense of ennobling unison you will feel. You will feel the "Truth" in another being.

VI
SENTIENCE

*A hermit shedding isolation to
a domain not so inclined.*

SENTIENCE
ABILITY TO REASON, THINK AND FEEL; CONSCIOUSNESS

To everyone this Key is given;
Is it a right, or Blessing granted
to each upon their own creation?
In the annals of Eternity
certain of its own existence
from the Great Causation,
a Consciousness is Born
anew in every Mind of Man.
Whereupon the Woman speaks,
"I Am," too, a Soul like you!
To simply know that we exist;
The Gift and Key that we've been given.
And so, poised at life's beginning,
searching for this Sojourn's Meaning
the fog of life does obfuscate
this Path we seek to navigate.
And here we probe,
and there, behold,
clues that may have been foretold;
A hermit shedding isolation
to a domain not so inclined.
Eloquent now the conversation,
the rapture rising now sublime;
I think I see;
I know I Am;
Cogito,[1] ergo sum.
But understanding this to be,
I know now

---

1 Cogito Ergo Sum: I think, therefore I am

that I know naught;
For finding Him with just this key
is not so facile as I thought.
And as we struggle to discern,
where does infinity reside;
We fail the final test, to look
for consciousness inside.
The neglected Altar of Divinity
is here and everywhere;
Noble protest finds no hearing
in souls who know not what they are.
For this Key is for each
a different Gate to open
to its own Elysium;[2]
All from the mind of the "I Am."
I Shed my Shield in final surrender and
open my Impassioned Heart;
This Cloistered Soul
now breathes New Life;
This Key, this Gift
has made it so.

---

[2] In Greek mythology, the home of the blessed after death; Heaven

We exist. We live. I Am. You are. To simply be able to say those words whose origins are in the Mind is something we hardly note, yet our ability to understand that we exist is perhaps the highest order of Blessed Burden we could have received. There was a time in the distant past, when a single, unique, first of its kind human, understood that it existed. That first Being that thought **"what will happen to me, if anything, and where will I go, if anywhere, when this existence as I now know it, comes to an end"?** This was the beginning of the search for Purpose and Meaning. That seminal moment is when it became a "being," which is what the word defines; Being. Today we ignore and take for granted that we know that we exist. But it was not always so. The great philosopher, Rene Descartes wrote in The Principles of Philosophy in 1644, "Cogito, ergo sum," (Latin) which means "I think, therefore I am" and can also be interpreted as "I am thinking, therefore I exist." Thinking about your existence, in and of itself, confirms that there is a "you" or "I" to have the thought itself. Even if you doubted your existence you would be confirming your existence by knowing that you are thinking your doubts. This provides the basis for other knowledge. But let's "cogitate" about that first "inspired" human Being who somehow had that elevated thought where existence…being, was grasped and understood. Think about you being that first human that had such a thought and feeling. Was it overwhelming or was it just another day? The revelation of Self must have been a glorious one, as it was the first of its kind in humanity as we know and understand it.

But it is a Blessed Burden because while it is a Gift, it is also that which triggers our search for Meaning and Purpose. I know now that I am. Now I need to know Why I am. I also want to know Who I am and Who made me and also When and How. Remember perception? Now the greatest gift can become the greatest burden, and so the Conundrum goes.

Consciousness is the "God Key."

We each get one, perhaps one different from another. Each of us with that key needs only find the right door. Find **your** Path.

VII
A BREATH OF ADONAI

I wipe a tear from a face that now exists in Another Self, not here.

A BREATH OF ADONAI

Existence.
Pure and Eternal;
Enslaved in its own history.
The cosmological framework,
and…Its Superior Other Self;
That which in shallowness seems the lesser,
in a reality, ethereal [1] embraces the physical.
Recognizing its power exceeds our capacity,
but Sweet and brief are the Glimpses we feel.
Overwhelming, indiscernible, fleeting.
Energy overcomes me as
my body disappears.
I wipe a tear from a face that now exists
in Another Self, not here.
It arises in me in a way I cannot comprehend;
Then…Enlightenment;
The glimpse is in my grasp
to see and understand.
I feel the breath of
"Adonai."
My body is vapor and Thought;
Countless particles of Existence.
Now, my body is here again.
Adonai has breathed into this self;
And I have come to know the
White Wave.

---

1 Extremely elegant, delicate or exquisite in a manner that seems too perfect for this world

Inspiration and Illumination come when least expected. You may be looking in the heavens at the countless stars and galaxies and become overwhelmed with an understanding of the existence of the Eterniverse. Perhaps a scientist seeking an answer to an unsolvable question gets an inspiration that helps to solve the riddle. Holding your newborn child is a miracle unto itself, both inspiring and incredulous. One of my sons, David, finds his Heart and Soul in his beloved dogs and finds a different level of understanding in them. My other son, Joshua, finds his Enlightenment in thinking.

God gives us glimpses of Enlightenment. You may have had such an experience where you "felt" everything or knew in advance what was going to happen for just a fleeting moment, then it was gone. You see and know things that a temporal being doesn't normally know or see like feeling the growth of a flower or becoming the flow in a stream. Those brief views into Transcendence open our window of understanding and our Listening frequency to the understanding that there is another existence. That there is something else. Why are these visions so brief? I think it is because It would be so overwhelming that we could not absorb Its fullness in this dimension and in this temporal life. But it is a message to those who would take time to listen. It is your treasure; your Purpose and Meaning veiled within.

VIII
SEATTLE WOMAN

…in that pain and burden she was
Fortitude and Courage.

SEATTLE WOMAN

Her arrival seemed so ordinary.
Just another person climbing aboard the bus.
Another day in the life…
Me, going to another deal.
Pensive. What might this day bring?
Nothing out of the normal happenings.
Then I "saw" her,
and I will never forget her.
She was sitting uncomfortably
on the shuttle seat, body tilted slightly
and somewhat off balance
as if in some pain.
Her back was slightly bowed
it seemed from many years of toil,
And from life.
Her clothes were spent as was her bag.
She stared blankly through the windows
and right through all around her.
No one was present to her
Here and now.
She did not see me with her eyes
But she spoke to me without
the feebleness of words,
in a different language.
The language of the Spirit.
She did not know that I saw her
And felt her burden;
It made me heavy of body and soul;
It was palpable inside me
as my mind and body tried to share
some manner of strength with her.
Her ashen gaze revealed but one thing…

"The obligation to keep moving…"
Somehow, keep moving.
But in that pain and burden
she was Fortitude and Courage,
now having to arise and
move toward the day at hand.
Everlasting is the fear, until
Enlightenment takes us and spares us.
I have pain for her to this day.
But should I? Many times
things are not what they seem.

In the frenzied flow of our lives we are seldom mindful of hidden messages. These messages are present everywhere. They are revealing and instructive if we but listen for them. We are so dependent on the verbal and visual that we ignore the underlying intuitive language that has nothing to do with spoken words or physical sight. The world opens to those who learn the language of the Soul.

Why too is it that some things, some people, some events, even things like aromas and flavors make such a vivid impression on us that they stay with us forever? Sometimes they are seemingly insignificant, yet there they are decades later, unforgettable. What is the construct of your Mind that not only allows that to occur but causes it to occur? Is there is meaning or purpose in that event? Was it coincidental or purposeful? Is anything a coincidence or does every single thing have a purpose? Though it is still in memory, why do we ignore it?

Something, somewhere, some Grand Thought may be sending you a message. Learn the language of listening and you will be aware and in awe of what the world tells you.

IX
MEMENTO MORI

*…my protest is in vain, for my Heart,
my Soul, my Mind you have sequestered.
Why did I have to love you so?*

MEMENTO MORI
REMEMBER YOU WILL DIE

*In the darkness of the Universe
a new Light stirs to Life.
Unknown perhaps, for it is in the past
but it flickers in my Soul
though I know it not.
Yes, to Life it springs, this new Creation,
set to Sail on life's new paths;
It chooses Radiance over darkness,
becoming One with her Creator.
And in this Soulful Flame unending,
with another Soul she makes a pact;
To an Eternity together,
bound to one another,
to bring forth breath to their own Creation.
From the Realm of the Great One
comes this Momentary Mind;
Those created first
now give birth to a new being…
and they too liberate their seed.
From thence I came to be, from her;
And now that Light is in me.
From Mother to Mother
to this humble soul.
You are "In Lak Ejh,"
"My other self"
Why do I have to love you so?
Knowing that Painful Passion must also come.
But my protest is in vain, for
my Heart, my Soul, my Mind
you have sequestered.
Why did I have to love you so?*

But painful as this day may be,
I cannot trade this eternal embrace
that made a grandson out of me.
Do I fear death?
Or fear life more?
This day, it makes my soul now cloistered
see that both are Eloquent Transcendence;
From birth to passing, then to
Renaissance.
And so this Fire that's in my Heart
consumes all fear forever more.
Your liberation back to the Light;
Light of Mind that is Eternal.
Oh! Philothea![1] You opened your arms
to take back life that dwells in me.
I search deep into that final blessing;
Memento Mori...
Remember, we all must die,
Reminds this soul.
I look beyond this window
feeling but not seeing you;
Tears flow from an impassioned heart
as two hands touch my shoulders.
I'm awakened by this loving touch and
the Celebration now continues.
I now ponder this anew;
Enthéos made me love you so.

---

1 Philothea: From St Francis de Sales 1609 writings, Introduction to the Devout Life; meaning "Love, or Lover of God."

It has been said that life without death is imponderably meaningless. This life is precious to us because we know it will end. We love even though we know that someday there will be the pain of loss. Again, we find that one cannot exist without the other as with so many other things in life. In many ways the intensity of the pain is commensurate with the intensity of the love.

Life and death; isolation and companionship; hardship and success. We focus on the beginning and end of these things but seldom on the "Now" of them. The Past breeds regret and the Future engenders fear. Yet the past, present and future are synchronous and therefore we should focus on the Path between the beginning and the end. It is in fact the very pain, isolation and hardship that give meaning to Life, Friendship and Success. They are intimately connected by the pursuit, the longing, and the toil and cannot be separated. While loving your parents, spouse, children or grandparents, vow to enjoy the present experience instead of past troubles and the fear of the future. When faced with hardship, recognize that you have an unfair advantage over those who have never experienced hardship and live that part of life fully and without regret, self punishment or fear. It is tempering you and preparing you to enjoy the fulfillment of your goal. If you are alone, that supposed void in your life is the seasoning for your eventual companionship and its ultimate enjoyment. There can be no void or emptiness without the knowledge that something can fill it. The anticipation must be as sweet as the fulfillment. There is wonder in uncertainty. Embrace the anticipation.

Promise yourself to embrace, enjoy and revel in ALL of life's moments, journeys and paths. All of them together make up the Grand Design, a Grand recipe that contains all of the ingredients for your Book of Life. Your life would not be complete without them.

X
PERDITION

The loveliness of Grand Thoughts, of worthy codes and Noble Purpose was soon to have a virulent and defiant spirit in its midst, so that the Sanctity of His Heavenly Bounty was but a whisper.

PERDITION
DAMNATION

In the course of human endeavor
we find the Embodiment of Soaring Illumination.
From Lao Tzu to Mother Teresa
both following, and showing The Way.
Out of the wilderness sprouted sentience and ambition
crawling forth from a vestigial past;
First to give Ancient Voice to primal thought,
then putting to written symbols what was the Scribner's
lasting message to the future.
Buildings too; pyramids, palaces and shrines
all grasping desperately
to reach the Firmament
and its Existential Artisan…
unreachable on stone and mortar.
There too was a Great Awakening
of Pythagoras[1] and Fibonacci;
Albert and Isaac and Leonardo
came too soon for some it seemed.
Ah!! Yes!! The magic of science, numbers
and measures, set us free, or so it seemed,
To live in a confinement
Woven in the Mind.
So too did Hammurabi's Code[2],
The Decalogue and Common Law
attempt to guide is through
the devastating torrent of ambition.
And the palate of desire for more,
grew into kinship with
the voices of darkness.
How the Purity of Intent morphed into the

---

1 Pythagoras…Leonardo: Great scientists, mathematicians, physicists and artists in history
2 Hammurabi's Code…Decalogue: The Code of Hammurabi dating to the 18th century BCE and the Ten Commandments

Great Race to no where is too,
a great conundrum.
The loveliness of Grand Thoughts,
of worthy codes and Noble Purpose
was soon to have a virulent and defiant spirit
in its midst, so that the Sanctity of
His Heavenly Bounty was but a whisper.
Reverence and Peace and Word
did mighty battle with ardent, unchained
and insidious motive.
Who are the children of this
unabated and unbridled fervor?
What has spawned from these
denizens of darkness?
Conquest and domination!
Servitude unwelcome to those who toil
for their earthly masters;
Labour born of bloodstained whips and cuffs;
Poverty to build the treasures of the crown;
Hard bread, the fuel of labour honest;
And we curse them all
as if devoid of Dignity,
and worship at the altar of decadence.
Where be the faint defense from
cultured class of those so trodden?
It is veiled in the approbation of ease and comfort
granted by the king, the state,
the royal robes of war and all their bounty.
Does not the widow suffer
as does the orphan?...
No less diminished be they ally or opponent.
Let us now know that the price
for earthly treasure

is paid with betrayal of the Universal Mind.
But do we comprehend this path?
No, not path! This unrelenting
fate with Megiddo?[3]
Alia Iacta Est! The die is cast!
This crossing of the Rubicon provides no retreat.
Shall we then say that
it is the natural progression of things?
Is it us?
That the Primeval Atom came to this end?
Think deeply…
Unchain your Mind.
Find Enthéos in the recesses of your Soul.
Awaken once again
to the Filigree of Life!
Be gone from me,
Perdition!
Depart from me now!
I choose the Fragrant Tapestry of
Eternal Mind.

---

3 Armageddon

We consider ourselves so evolved that we see ourselves as the prudent master of this earthly domain. We know what is best for all things be they plants, animals or other humans. From this superior position we decide who and what lives and dies. The mob in the Colosseum would decide who lived or died in the arena all to satisfy some primal urge for a spectacular public death.

And what of unbridled ambition? Governments and leaders, whether Egyptian, Roman, Chinese, Aztec or American decided that they needed to subdue some culture, tribe or nation; destroy it and all who made a life there, or in the alternative, harvest the vanquished peoples and land for their own benefit. And the citizens allow themselves to become stirred to nationalism or jingoism, all for pride in country and worse, sometimes in the name of God. Domination and destruction ensue and "to the victor belongs the spoils." Yet I have often noted that peoples get along fine, while governments thrive on war. And who reaps the fatal benefits of such excursions? Soldiers in the prime of life, maimed for life or dead; their fathers and mothers, wives, siblings and children left without them. Widows and orphans on both sides pay the ultimate price, yet victory is claimed and celebrated while lives and families are destroyed in the name of domination and conquest. And what exactly did the widows and orphans do to provoke the onslaught? Sadly, entire industries exist to support and promote discord and millions are handsomely rewarded in every manner, from employment to investments. What is it in our nature that thrives on this mental state? Whether a world war or someone's road rage mini war, it seems to be all about domination and exertion of will. How will it end? How **can** it end?

We have so much to offer and yet we take and grasp at all things not in our possession. Ultimately, all such efforts have been in vain and have left but veiled history fading into dust and no substantive lessons learned though we claim to have learned the lessons of history. Perhaps that is what makes us who and what we are.

But there are some who teach us what we **can** be if we will seek truth and listen. There is also much goodness and kindness in this world. We must find the balance between that which is beneficial and peacefully empowering and that which is degrading and dominating for the sake of success and accomplishment. Start by looking into your own life and seeking Balance and as a result, true Power.

XI
CUNUNDRUM

*Reaching, grasping, forever wanting…
that which binds us to this place. This impassioned
avocation has made us prisoners of our freedom.*

CONUNDRUM
A QUANDARY; DILEMMA; DIFFICULT QUESTION

Reaching, grasping, forever wanting;
In this world it is our passion
to create eternity in one lifetime.
Temporal is but a word; an idea
obfuscated by our earthly pleasures.
The drive; the push; the pressure;
Constant and inexorable[1] doings
of all things to lessen travails
and lengthen life… just a little more.
See, this is better, faster, bigger,
richer, easier or grander.
Now we're pleased, but not for long
and not so much as to stop the
incessant lacking and "just a little more."
And this all done in Freedom's name?
Liberation…the pursuit of ALL in frenzy
from work and time and space constrained,
and above all, from that nemesis, Death.
And yet we dance with this credo too;
That life to come in everlasting
is the purpose of the present realm.
That the purpose for Creation
is not for here and now,
but for the Eternal Treasure.
This we claim in eloquent prayer;
that He take us Home to Paradise.
And we claim still more…
That we surrender to His will.
But what true aim is cloistered there?

---

1 Impossible to stop or prevent

*For Truth would not be so inclined
as to concur with this elixir.
Enter now the Great Conundrum.
Are you now ready for the Revelation
or shall we hide in the shadows
of our Liberation, bound by chains?
All we seek; what we see and taste and hear;
Health and hearth and all things human,
that which leads us to Utopia?
But its meaning here is "No Place,"
but few there are who know its meaning.
Reaching, grasping, forever wanting,
that which binds us to this place.
This impassioned avocation has
made us prisoners of our freedom.
Clinging, praying for more life;
Just one more day
in defiance of the Divine Dialogue.
But why? If that's the purpose,
to Him to go,
doth one resist the final consummation?
That final gasp of breath so dear,
fades into the mist,
but not without resistance.
Would not a Soulful Surrender
be more gallant?
True Emancipation! And
freed from these desires.
These erstwhile freedoms fog the soul
and fail to see the Flame Unending.
Just one more breath…*

Just one more…
Reaching, grasping, forever wanting.
"But why?" Asks the Great Elohim.
"Approach the Light.
Release your Soul to me.
Flow to me like Honey Sweet.
I Am yours and you are Mine."

I submit to you this question;

Have we really achieved the freedoms we so desperately seek, or have we created an earthly and temporal prison where as Patrick Henry so ardently voiced,

"Is life so dear or peace so sweet as to be purchased at the price of chains and slavery?"

It is an interesting human trait or condition that our entire history is an inexorable progression to achieve an improved physical, temporal condition. We have changed and manipulated the world and our lives within it by "improving" virtually everything; housing, agriculture, foods, medicines, transportation, communication, language, civil order, laws, printing, arts, sciences and countless other elements of our then, and current existence. In and of themselves, these are not bad or evil things. These efforts have contributed greatly to an improved human existence and enjoyment of our temporal lives. That is a good thing. The most humble tract home today would have been an incomprehensible luxury in the not so distant past. 10,000 years ago a primitive hand inscribed symbol would travel by foot over a thousand miles and over a thousand years. Today a billion words travel across the globe in a nano second. Humans are unique in this regard. Inventions that spring from the mind and their physical manifestations (the improvements) help satisfy basic human traits such as a desire to make life easier and more comfortable to live and also to provide pleasure and security.

These things are also driven by an insatiable need for freedom. Freedom from travails, hard manual labor, difficulties, disorder, famine, transience and temporariness, disease and almost any form of limitation including time and distance. It is difficult to argue that we have not been successful. Again, these are not bad things. Why would we want to live like people lived even in the Middle Ages? Yet for many, these things remain basically unchanged in today's world.

Certainly residents of the Earth ten thousand years ago would think they were in a different world if they experienced ours. And they would be right.

For most of us, to voluntarily choose between this "life so dear" and the grim reaper, is non sequitur.[2] It does not follow. For most people, to live a longer life and to enjoy more is the ultimate freedom from limitations. Or so it seems. Because we are so bound by this desire, because we have invested the sum total of human progress and achievement in this idea, we do not want to leave. We want more time, even if just a little more, despite the knowledge that we inevitably must and will leave this place. This uniquely human and temporal construct here on Earth has made us prisoners of the very freedoms we created. I am reminded of Emily Dickenson's comment regarding death; "Because I could not stop for Death, he kindly stopped for me."

In the movie, "Meet Joe Black" which is based on the book "Death Takes a Holiday," he, being Death incarnate, lives in the world for some time while preparing to take his next "client," Bill, and experiences all of the pleasures of life including a forbidden relationship with Bill's daughter, with whom he falls in love. When he is finally confronted with the fact that he must depart this world back to the realm of Death to take Bill with him, even he, Death itself, says in his own mini jeremiad,[3] "I don't want to go!" He felt this way solely because he had the experience of life here on Earth. But he knew he had to go, just as we know that we too must "go." In an interesting turn of events, Bill, for whom Death came, announces he is ready to go, but Death itself

---

[2] A conclusion or statement that "does not follow" logically from a previous statement.
[3] A long mournful complaint or lamentation; a list of woes and troubles.

says it does not want to leave yet. In this same movie, Bill who is Death's target says something very unusual at his last birthday party. "…I don't want anything more," he says. Yes, he had a life with the greatest of luxuries but it would be stunning nonetheless to hear someone state that and mean it.

So we ask, "What instruction can we receive from this?"

Perhaps we would not exist as a species if we were not so aggressive.

Do we have things or do things have us?

Perhaps we could have some satisfaction, pleasure and peace with less, rather than more.

Perhaps we should seek Balance in all things and in that Balance, have true Power.

Perhaps your life can be an example of how to live a life in Balance.

XII
EMBRACE

*In the lamentation of the mourning dove
the Great One beckons me to follow.*

EMBRACE

*A subtle wind blows
And I feel His Breath;
Luminous Stars in Noble Regalia
bring his Graceful Gaze upon me.
Droplets of rain wash my face;
It is The Master
shedding a tear.
The breeze, a tree and Terra,
a Trinity of Sacred Intimacy.
Sunlit sky or clouds afire, are
but a stage to the Great One.
Forest, ocean and mountaintop are
the earthly Domain of their Creator.
A fresh rose blooming, and its thorns too;
A reminder of His Love and Justice.
Desert sands in Silent Grandeur;
Pure of Soul, the Divine Essence.
Creatures countless paying tribute;
Sublime Prayer to the Great Spirit.
Earth and sun and moon and stars;
Celestial Heartbeat of the Prince.
And what of time and space eternal?
Light of Mind is bound not by them.
Even stone and air, fire and water
are humble servants of Genesis.
Man of Clay and Woman, his Partner;
Reflections of the Highest Order.
Mind and soul and spirit human;
Fleeting glimpse of the Transcendent.
In the lamentation of the mourning dove
the Great One beckons me to follow.
Resplendent Rainbow…Majestic Doorway*

*to the Kingdom and the Crown.
For if we question
"What's my purpose?"
Know that at this all Embracing Altar
each of these is Divine Presence;
All together are but One.
For Noble Purpose all were made;
The Great Amen in everything.
In this Crescendo of Creation
one does not exist
without the other Being.*

We can choose what see and hear in everything. For most people who are not tuned in to the frequency of life and the Eterniverse, most things are just noises and nuisances. We fail to listen to the dialogue that is most meaningful; the conversation that informs us that all things are related because they all originate from one Grand Causation. Present yourself with a Divine gift by pausing to see and listen to the sights and sounds of life whatever they may be. Take pleasure in the Grandeur of Creation instead of passing blindly through its midst and many wondrous portals. And when you do, feel the uniqueness of your Self as a Singular Being as it becomes a part of Everything. Plotinus, a later student of Plato wrote, "Everything in the universe is connected just as they are each and all parts of one single organism and all put together are part of and make up the 'Single Mystical One', from which everything originated and to which all things will return."

The Universe does not exist without you Being in it.

The Universe could not exist without you in it. If it could have, it would have; but it couldn't, and it doesn't.

That is how important and interrelated all things are in the Eterniverse.

XIII
VITAM AETERNAM

And what of all eternity before you?
A Timeless Tomb of Script…
unknown but to the Great Causation.

VITAM AETERNAM
LIFE ETERNAL

Poised on the precipice of
yesterday and tomorrow,
we see the history of this life
that we think we know.
We know less of that which
may yet come to existence…
Perhaps a void, or more.
But the Heart of the Past,
without beginning,
And the Soul of the Future,
without end,
escape understanding.
This Universal Absence…and Presence,
clothed in isolation and deception
deceive our desires in primeval masquerade.
Is your history fact, fiction or truth?
How can one truly know?
It is the fog of regret that
inhabits the Mind of the Past
like a Euphoric Impassioned Scream of a
memory harbored in its pantheon.
And what of all eternity before you?
A Timeless Tomb of Script…
unknown but to the Great Causation.
And now like Janus[1]
we look ahead in Pursuit of History
as a sepulchre awaits its new servant.
Dreams and Love and Life
and Beauty fleeting,
all lurking and conspiring, fool us

---

[1] The Roman god of beginnings and transitions who had two faces, one looking to the past and one looking to the future. The month of January is derived from Janus. January looks back upon the prior year and forward to the new year.

*in preparation for the Final Test,
to see which lives and gives hope anew.
And yet we rest now
at the confluence of these two pretenders,
Past and Future.
And the Harmony of these two strands
startles me into the "Now."
For "Now" is what we have,
and even so, it's gone before we grasp it.
What shall we make of this Enigma?
Perhaps it is the human frailty
of being bound by all things measured.
Seconds ticking…hours wasting;
Days gone by and how much life is left to live.
The speed of light in time and space,
an effort vain and futile.
Let us rather watch a plant grow,
hold an ancient hand and feel its history;
Feel the Sun and breathe once more.
Breathe Life Eternal into your Soul
for it is Now and it is Here, while
frail words will disappear.
But your Enthéos, your God within,
Always Was and Always IS and Always Will Be.
In this Domain of Wonderment
the answer to this query;
The "who" and "why" and "when" of us,
is seated at the Banquet of the Present.
Vitam Aeternam, hidden in the Self
can veil itself no longer,
for my Soul now sees this Revelation.
It lives Now, in Life Eternal.*

If in your Book of Life it was written that you would live forever here in this world, would you feel elation or would you feel fear? Would you want to live forever? Or is it the knowledge that we will pass into Infinity that gives this life meaning? We preoccupy ourselves with the past and the future so much that we forget that the only thing we have is "now." Did you ever think that eternity cannot be measured either? It is simply a word to express in human thought that which we do not comprehend in this existence, whether past or future. Seconds and centuries mean nothing to time. Time exists independent of them and of our concept of time. Imagine being in a paradise in eternity that you know will never have an end and therefore you will always be there. What makes that horrifying and intolerable is that we would always be aware that even in that paradise which we ostensibly desire, there would be no end to it. Why would it be intolerable? Because we think of time and space in terms of measurement. Seconds, minutes, hours, days, months, years, decades, and eons, without an end. Is there an end to the future? If there isn't, then in our human habit of measurement, we could never stop counting the passage of time. Infinity entails one more of something; one more inch or light year; one more second or one more Universe. Then one more.

When we leave this temporal world and become transformed to Spirit and Transcendence, there can be no time or space. That existence would not be bound by time and space and therefore would not be subject to measurement by our standards. That form of existence which is not bound by time and space is true Liberation.

Why not view the "now" as eternal life because now never passes? It is always with us here and now. And when we transcend this temporal world we will once again be in an infinite now of existence although its exact nature is incomprehensible to us. This part of our existence is also a part of Eternal Life. Take time now to live and feel the truly important things. See yourself as an Eternal Being on a journey through the physical domain which is also a precious gift for it reminds us of our past and future infinity.

XIV
LIBERATUS

What of this Man So deep transformed?
New Life, New Birth, New Light; Lux Eternus,
illumines his gaze; Pax Eternus, quiets his Soul.

LIBERATUS
LIBERATED; RELEASED

What of this man?
Mournful, painful, soul sequestered;
By his own hand has brought it forth.
He knows, he sees, now understanding.
The might of rule and law
now governs and gives orders,
now keeps him here
to spend some life in captive space;
Currency and time both compete
to harvest his being in this place, while
clemency is cost to those with keys.
But what of this Man do we not see?
'Tis more than those who stake a claim
to profit from his Life now stolen.
This Man IS Man!
Robbed not now of the One
to whom he kneels.
In the Sanctuary of his Soul,
there dwells his Renaissance.
New Life, New Birth, New Light;
Lux Eternus,[1] illumines his gaze;
Pax Eternus,[2] quiets his Soul.
What of this Man
So deep transformed?
Listening for the Keys of Freedom
so when those profiteers are finished,
to Home and hearth he quick departs
and leaves behind those others waiting.
What of this Man?
Twice a Lazarus;
Born anew and hungry no more.

---

1 Eternal Light
2 Eternal Peace

This is a story about redemption. This man knows he has sinned against the state and has repented and found peace, but the system cares little about those things. What the system cares about is maintaining the status quo with those who profit from this man's bondage. But the world sees this man in only one way; as a criminal, even after he has served his time.

So many times we see a person solely in their situation or current state of being and we fail to see the real person behind the veil. Regardless of a person's supposed condition or those things by which society defines that person we must always be aware that a real life and a real person lies beyond the judgment. It has happened countless times since time immemorial that one judges another's life and when given the opportunity to know that person, the opinions disappear and you find the real person.

Everyone in this world struggles with something, but many keep their struggles to themselves. They have a lifetime of experiences, loves, losses, happiness, agony and emotions. Because we are creatures that have learned to survive, we fight through the seas of desperation so many times present in our lives. No one really knows your life and most people are so busy with their own lives that they rarely take time to know the lives of others. But mostly, we survive and win the battles and live another day. But there is a real person inside you that you wish others knew instead of the one they think they know. There is Redemption, Reconciliation and Forgiveness to consider.

Ultimately you must find yourself and know yourself. Your Enthéos. That is what makes you Powerful and Undefeatable and gives you true Liberation.

XV
REPENTANCE

*Oh Enthéos! Come to me! Guide my Path through
Paradise Lost. And if it be in Your Mind's Gift,
set this table for me once again. Knowing that
I did not see, I look inside to find true treasure.*

REPENTANCE

*Perchance this heart does still hold dear
after time and space have made their stand,
that this repentant soul so broken
sees what was so close, now from afar.
Yet there is Sacred Sacrifice in both
defiant spirits jousting for survival.
Ardor Noble and unabated, in respect of
Veritas, a Truth laid bare, once buried deep.
If only I had glimpsed this future of
devastation to the Soul and Spirit.
Justified no more can this arrangement be;
Ordered, yes, but now rejected.
Soulful anguish seems now eternal,
hindered solely by the Mind.
Unrequited Love's now silenced this
altered realm of new Existence.
Oh Enthéos! Come to me!
Guide my Path through Paradise Lost.
And if it be in Your Mind's Gift,
set this table for me once again.
Knowing that I did not see,
I look inside to find true treasure.
You are now my Banquet, Enthéos.*

We have all lost loved ones in one form or another. While the person or relationship was living, we may have understood and respected them for the gift they were to us and in some cases, continue to be. Sometimes perhaps we just went through the motions and gave fleeting recognition to the real Meaning and Purpose they brought into our lives. Many times relationships are difficult and challenging. Someone once confided in me that "it's hard to be married." It could be said that it is hard to be in any relationship for a long term whether as parent, child, brother, sister, spouse or employment.

So often however, when that relationship or person is absent we begin to understand its importance. We gain a kind of Clarity that we did not have before. We see it through a different lens or perspective. We gain appreciation. In a very strange way, that preserves the relationship and perhaps in a better manner than before.

Stop and think about the people in your life today. Each one is a Special Gift that you should honor and respect. The Pursuit of Happiness, Meaning and Purpose is hidden in plain sight and we can harvest their bounty if we but wash away the fog of ignorance and ingratitude that often permeate our lives.

XVI
LAPSIT EX CAELIS

*To me here, an open Heart, expecting not this
Special Treasure, provides this Soul a sudden start,
my Spirit filled beyond all measure.*

LAPSIT EX CAELIS
IT FELL FROM THE HEAVENS

We live our lives in Hope and fear
expecting gifts from God above,
and so He sends us something Dear,
a Symbol of His Love.
Then when our Minds are far adrift
thinking not of His Good Graces,
heaven sent arrives this Gift,
to where? Of all earth's places?
To me here, an open Heart,
expecting not this Special Treasure,
provides this Soul a sudden start,
my Spirit filled beyond all measure.
I thank you for this Angel sent,
a Message loud and clear.
That moment when I seemed so spent,
adrift no more, Your Voice I hear.

Somewhere, somehow…something, a Universal Intelligence, has prepared a path in your Book of Life the contents of which are unknown to you. How excruciating and utterly without Meaning and Purpose would it be to know with certitude every chapter, verse and word of your path in your Book of Life? What would be the worth of living a life whose every twist and turn, every nuance, you already knew in advance? It is the "not knowing" that drives that indomitable human trait of pushing forward in the face of the unknown and fuels the pursuit of meaning and purpose, including things that can lead you into the jaws of the Dragon. When drowning in that sea of desperation one questions if and when it will ever come to an end.

Then, the dove approaches your troubled ark and you sense hope in the tempest. The clouds break, the sun shines and the Universal Intelligence sends you something Precious whose loveliness is only enhanced by your past travails.

And so it is with not only surviving, but thriving on those events and conditions in our lives that present the most difficult "opportunities." The partaking of the banquet that is to come is seasoned more by the difficult path to its realization. Learn to take the power from difficulties and make it your own. Problems become powerless against you when you take away their power. Thus you become undefeatable.

And…keep your heart open for that Special Treasure.

XVII
LUMINOUS

*…my luminescent messenger sows its seed in my Spirit.
I see the Truth now…Now I know.*

LUMINOUS

A parched and naked land,
this Soul, this Heart, this Spirit;
Needing but not knowing that
the Truth in myriad forms appears.
Nourishment? or Devastation?
The Soul the Truth expecting,
The Heart, the Truth rejecting; the
Spirit bathed and clothed within it.
But it is an illusion; a fiction;
For I look but do not see
because this illusion is a shadow
that starves my understanding and
feeds my wanton way, yet I am famished.
And my knowing is now too, an illusion.
What I understand is now not truth,
But my eyes, set apart, reveal the Truth.
I failed to behold the Angiras,[1]
the Luminous Being He set at my table.
The Master knew I would demur;
That the delusion would reign.
The Grail was in hand, yes,
but not in Mind, Soul or Heart.
And upon hearing Her pronouncement
I saw that I was blind, then did not hear.
This travail I wish not on Sisyphus,[2]
for in his deed was purpose more
than my feeble hopeless mirage.
But the Master bequeathed
to this longing Soul
the passion to learn to see,
to know, to understand

---

1 A sage or celestial being
2 In Greek mythology, a king who was punished by being forced to roll an immense boulder up a hill only to watch it roll back down, repeating this task forever

*that when the Banquet is set
once again before me,
this will be Nourishment,
not devastation or blindness.
Alma receiving Truth
with its siblings, Heart and Spirit.
Open Alma cures this ill
and parched and naked land.
Now the guiding Angiras,
my luminescent messenger
sows its seed in my Spirit.
I see the Truth now…Now I know.*

The Master sets a bountiful table before us. Yet we take for granted that these are all blessed gifts. We rush through Life and fail to notice that every single thing, even seemingly insignificant things in our day to day lives are part of the fullness of the recipe. We think we are grateful, but are we really? Or are we trapped in a hopeless fiction? So many times the focus is not on the so called positives but on the negatives. But all of life's experiences, even those we are conditioned to consider as bad or negative, are part of the deal of Life. We fool ourselves into certain beliefs and refuse to see more deeply into things and ideas. We "buy in" to conventional thinking and deprive ourselves of seeing a different and plentiful world.

Things cannot always go your way. Your Book of Life has interesting detours, hurdles, hills and mountains, valleys and roadblocks along with joy, love, contentment and Peace. Your Book of Life would not be complete without all of Life's experiences. Learn to see and feel your life as a unique, "one of a kind" in the Eterniverse journey. Why? Because it is exactly that. Out of billions of people, there is no other human in the past, present or future that has lived, or will live a life exactly like yours. That is something to be embraced and honored; that you have something no other person will ever have or has ever had. That singularity is overwhelming and should fill your Spirit with joy and gratitude. You are genuinely unique. One of a kind.

In this journey there are Luminous messengers that veil themselves in the form of seemingly non descript people (like The Seattle Woman), events or things, but they are there and you will notice them if you stop and recognize what is all around you. Look past the obvious and see beneath the superficial. See the Angiras that is guiding you through your Book of Life. Then you will know.

XVIII
GRATIA PLENA

*For we have more than we can know
regardless of our life's condition, Gratia Plena,
the arc and bow against the Soul's perdition.*

GRATIA PLENA
FULL OF GRACE

*As this delusion envelops me
I look for Truth, I search, I find
the Real Essence that is He,
the Light of Eternal Mind.
Yet if we pause to listen
to the din and to the Soul,
revelation we now christen
on this Sacred Sancta shoal.
Thus, is our duty to discern
from that which is perception,
foremost now we must adjourn
'gainst all that is deception.
For we have more than we can know
regardless of our life's condition,
Gratia Plena, the arc and bow
against the Soul's perdition.
The fog of loss and of despair
clouds our knowing of Enthéos,
but when partaking of God's Share
we come grateful to our Deus.
The Pow'r in me is bursting forth,
Gratia Plena unabated;
Gratitude's my Holy Shout,
for me, to Him, I was Created.*

It seems that we have difficulty defining "Grace." Spiritual cultures the world over, describe Grace in many ways. Grace has been defined as the Divine Gift and The Ultimate Key required for spiritual self realization. To every spiritual being, Grace is something of the Soul; something so powerful yet intangible. Can you feel it when you have Grace? How does Grace manifest itself in your daily Path? How might it feel if you didn't have Grace? Can you see and feel Grace in others?

Perhaps gratitude is the appropriate prayer when contemplating Grace. It is a Sacred State that comforts us in despair and protects us from perdition. It is The Great Causation within.

XIX
ENCLAVE

*That which screams that it is Truth…
by its very shout deems itself devoid.*

ENCLAVE

As I walk in trepidation to the gates of Liberation
I sense my heart beats at a different pace.
Nourishment now has a different meaning
to a palate that was lost in the mist of memory.
Phobos and Diemos; Fear and Terror both,
make their brief appearances, unfrocking Faith.
Enthéos wraps its Loving care onto my Soul
crushing doubters and invaders from my Mind.
My Listening now has a new frequency; fine tuned
and set to all new sounds and thoughts.
What is here and now is known, but painful.
What might be is simply "What might be."
A billion universes of possibilities
each driven by one single choice that is made
in the Matrix of the Mind.
This is a bankrupt world and existence
though in my Path I feel
I have harvested some good here.
And as this journey, Path and travail come to end,
I see the riches it has shown and brought me.
How shall we understand the "how" and the "why"?
The "how" was long ago determined;
The "why" now startles my heart.
To be made naked of all once held so dear…
and if this punishment is all that comes
from past transgressions,
my gratefulness is profound,
for a darker place well could have been.
Now as I set the preparation for departure
I see those I shall see no more.
For some it matters; for others, not.
And what is it that I take with me?

It's the Listening for the Language of the Soul.
The Language of Eloquence that dwells with God.
What Clarity of Inner Vision I have been given!
That which screams that it is Truth…
by its very shout deems itself devoid.
"Caras vemos, Corazones no sabemos";
"We see the face, but we know naught the heart."
That which preaches an unveiling,
weakens at the Throne of Truth and Humility.
Now I come nearer the gatekeeper
knowing certain that I do not know
my Book of Life as it awaits its Scribner
to pen into it those Paths that live even now.
How wonderful is the not knowing.
It is the Effervescence of Existence;
The Meaning and Purpose we seek.
For what a punishment it would be
to know fully each page, chapter and verse
of your Book of Life.
Damnation in a Book!!
No, thus I pace myself on this road
with Enthéos my Shield and Armor.
I hear the sound of keys…
they make my Soul both bristle and Rejoice.
Now I come to the Unapproachable Light.
I walk through the gates and feel the eyes
and hearts of those behind me
as their hopes and fears weigh upon us together.
I try to forget, yet I cannot do so
for This, and They,
have made this moment come to pass.

Uncertainty. Not knowing yet believing. Is it Faith or is it Fact? What will I do? Where will I go? Who will be there? What will happen? Who accompanies me on this Path? Am I joyous or am I angry? Am I excited or am I fearful? Can I ever let pass the experiences that have placed their mark on my Soul and in my Book of Life? I want to forget, but I must remember. I must remember. Pain and sorrow are the Seeds of Healing. They are the faitours[1] in our lives. But we transcend from pain to Power.

I have learned a new and enlightening language. An idiom that cannot be learned without the test that burns it into your Being. There is no other way. It is the trial that the Maker had written in the palm of His Hand but which was unknown to me. Now, it is unknown still what the Master Scribner has penned into my Book of Life. And I am grateful for this gift. The not knowing is the fuel that propels us to Meaning and Purpose. And I remember the wisdom of Ajahn Chah; "You are lost only if you forget who you really are."

Now I also remember that in this world, **precious things are precious because they are not forever.**

---

[1] Impostor

XX
GATHASPA

Knowledge was his music and he instructed me in its Instruments.

GATHASPA

I don't remember the day or moment I set eyes upon him,
nor that first wisp of loving and needing his presence,
for I was but a child.
But in my emergence to sentience
surely there was a passing from not knowing
to full awareness that he was, with my Mother,
the crucible of my existence and reason for being here.
As my Book of Life unfolded
Total devotion to him became the
sibling of abject dependence.
With these powerful emotions one can be lulled
into a kind of séance of servitude.
It must have been akin to mental seduction;
That my every act and thought was to please him.
And he read and knew my heart.
But there was a dark Solitude in his Soul
that seemed to chain his temperament
in a Prison of Unrealized Love;
A desperate fear of vulnerability.
The enigma was in the Knowing in my Soul
that his Love was Tethered to a Past
of Withered Expectations.
Yet in a quiet desperation not understood,
Redemption and Surrender
were my loyal companions.
His Redemption; My Surrender.
As my budding years yielded to Awakening
his unending threats of departure
which at first stung my Heart and Being
with a fear a child must never know,
transformed the deepest reaches of my Heart and Spirit
into acceptance…and apathy.

That which he perpetually sought by threat of absence
was now a Sad and Soulful Solitude.
Still, knowing he was Man and Father,
dissonance[1] succumbed to Love Unconditional.
He did not know that I understood,
but he did know my devotion and my Enthéos.
Thus, he Paved the Boundless Path to
the dialogue of learning.
This was his Loving and Eternal Gift to me;
Our Mental and Spiritual dance,
intimate and exhilarating.
And the Great Existential Essence prepared my
Spirit and Mind, my Heart and Soul
for the Harvest.
Appetite insatiable transformed a mere memory
to Virtual Knowing.
Knowledge was his music and he instructed me
in its Instruments.
And the now ancient attempts at preying on
an innocent heart, were sentenced to the Abyss.
Now, Mutual Emancipation from our mental constraints
ruled our new Brotherhood of the Mind.
I knew a day would arrive and make its pronouncement
that the River Styx[2] awaited its next passenger.
And so it came, and so it did.
The ancient chant and rite of Extreme Unction
seemed to Soothe his Soul to Tranquil Surrender.
Long lost terror tried to intervene, but
as he faced Elohim and paid his final debt,
both he and I released its embrace…
if only for a moment,

---

1 Lack of harmony; tension or clash resulting from two unsuitable elements.
2 To the ancient Greeks, the river that separated the world of the living from the world of the dead.

and instead embraced each other,
and this life, and the next.
As I held his precious head in my hands,
I saw and felt Him sail into the
Eternal Embrace.
Peace and Gratitude are now our blanket;
And Transcendence.
His name was Gaspar;
Gathaspa in Persian.
A Zoroastrian Priest;
One of the Magi, of the Three Wise Men.
He is Gathaspa, my Father.

Perhaps loving unconditionally is the only real answer to relationships with our parents which are sometimes complicated and challenging. Because of our humanity and also our Godliness, we experience everything from the most profound affection to exasperation at what seems to be their lack of understanding. But regardless of the chasm that might separate us, the robust bridges that span the disparate positions we assume are rarely destroyed beyond repair. Somehow, someway we remain spiritually connected. It can be no other way for just as all things are connected, this link is direct and immediate. There is something mighty and glorious about our parents that infuses our lives with the learning and eventually the Wisdom to live a meaningful life. It's just that we often don't realize it until later in life. There is an old saying: "The older I get, the smarter they get." Now, as we wear the robes of parents, we see and feel our parents from a different perspective and now Clarity of Vision comes into focus.

Each of these relationships has its own life. Its own sheet of music and orchestra. None of them is identical to another. So it was with my father and each of my siblings. Each one has had a different path in their Book of Life. In my path with him I had no regrets on the day he passed. Chuang Tzu wrote, "To wail and groan while my wife is sleeping (in death) would be to deny nature's sovereign law." It is in the natural order of things. That day, as I held his head in my hands, he passed and I saw into his eyes and Soul that at that very moment he was experiencing transcendence. It was a beautiful experience. I had Peace and I felt he did as well. Perhaps we should not fear death whether our own or that of those we love for it is the knowledge that we must pass someday that gives Meaning and Purpose to our love and passion for life.

Should we be afraid?

Should we have fear of anything?

Can you be undefeatable?

God within; Enthéos makes you undefeatable and gives you Balance and Power.

FINAL THOUGHTS

There are myriad elements in the path to becoming a Total Being. Finding and accessing the Power Within is the platform for reconciling the discordant portions of your life and evolving into the complete person you wish to become. The metamorphosis is not immediate nor should it be. The incremental achievements should be commensurate with the effort. It is a continuous effort that has no final celebration for to celebrate its arrival and accomplishment is itself, anathema.

Slowly, learning the arts of Inquiry and Listening, Personal Daily Reconciliation, Clarity and Purity of Intent, you will begin the transformative process of becoming a Total Being with Balance and Power. You will experience life in a most profound manner regardless of your financial and social status and perhaps despite your status. The thrilling part of your travels on this path is that you do not know what is written in your Book of Life. You are the scribner and it is being written even in this eternal now.

This path gives you the gift of being free from fear. Fear of failure, fear of loving someone, of not having enough, of not being liked, of not liking yourself, of dying, of circumstances you can't control, of what happens next. There is Power in releasing your grasp and allowing the God Key to open doors for you.

We journey together, you and I. I invite and welcome your inquiry and comments. Please share your thoughts and questions, comments and inquiries to vincent@lightofmind.us.

Thank you, and I remain as always your humble servant.

ABOUT THE AUTHOR

Vincent was born in the pastoral village of Tomé, New Mexico, a village 25 miles south of Albuquerque, New Mexico. His Spanish ancestors settled in the area in the early 1600's and were among the first settlers in Albuquerque's Old Town where he was raised. Brought up in the old ways of hard physical labor, he and his brothers made adobe bricks alongside their father through the summer months starting work at 4am and working until 8pm Monday through Saturday. The rest of the year was busy with Catholic school training under the tutelage of the Sisters of Charity and Jesuit priests, more hard labor after school and rising at 5:30 every morning to ring the old fashioned church bell to call people to Mass at 6:00 every morning where he served as an altar boy.

In business for himself since the age of 18, Vincent has been involved in business ventures as diverse as real estate development, commercial finance, acquisitions and divestitures, translations and negotiating settlements for adverse parties. He is widely considered a highly skilled negotiator who utilizes the finely honed art and science of inquiry and listening to reach settlements.

It was a decision regarding a loan transaction that resulted in a two year federal prison sentence for which he accepted full responsibility.

Vincent has mentored hundreds of people from a personal growth perspective and in business. He continues to mentor today and mentored several people while in prison.

His forthcoming books include:

(Finding) Balance & Power...in a troubled world

Becoming the Total Being

Free Will and Determinism. Confluence or Conflict?

Negotiating from Compassion.

If you would like to ask Vincent a question or contribute to his blog, such as your idea or interpretation of a particular writing, please do so at vincent@lightofmind.us.

Photograph by Victoria LeFevre

ABOUT THE ILLUSTRATOR

Imagine...for a moment...that our creativity and all that pertains to creativity is available at every moment. Now, imagine creating from this place. Imagine that the reservoir that is needed to create is always already here.

This is listening. Listening to what is available and responding to what is presented. Creativity moves into form through listening. Life moves from listening.

When Vincent and I meet, we listen, we inquire, we explore and inquire again. We inquire: how should my illustrations reflect the words Vincent so eloquently composed? We then listen to the pull of the One Mind... this is how the illustrations for the book *Enthéos* came forth.

Experiencing Vincent's presence: the wisdom he embodies and his unwavering conviction to point to truth in his writings, has become the basis of our kinship and the life force of my illustrations.

This life force is represented in my drawings of the revered papyrus plant. Each image is created to illustrate the life cycle of this ancient sacred plant. From seed to flower and back to seed again, with all its experiences and expressions along the journey. A true reflection of our human life cycle. Through this life force cycle, this body then returns to its origin.

As you journey through *Enthéos*, breathe in the layers of the passages and the art, and drink it all in!

In closing I present an invitation: An invitation to look within, to listen, listen to the always present pull, sense the portal and response.

Jeanine Christman Handell
www.jeaninechristman.com

THOUGHTS ON PAPYRUS

You will note a theme about papyrus and the papyrus plant throughout. It represents the cycle of life. Hold and feel a piece of papyrus paper and you will experience the first "talking paper" in the world as we know it. Thoughts that flowed from the mind of man could now be preserved for eons. Papyrus is a portal to the Life Force. It is organic and of the River Nile. It is Life. Through papyrus, sentience became tangible. It created a metamorphosis in humanity. It continues its ecstatic task today.

Vincent

I AM
EXODUS CHAPTER 13
VERSES 13-15

But Moses said to God (He who has no name),
"When I go to the Israelites and say to them,
'The God of your fathers has sent me to you,'
If they ask me 'what is His name'?
What am I to tell them?"
God replied, This is what you shall tell the Israelites

"I AM"

Sent me to you

"This is my name forever"

In Hebrew, this utterance is the source of the word/name

YAHWEH

The personal name of God to the Israelites.

www.ingramcontent.com/pod-product-compliance
Lightning Source LLC
Chambersburg PA
CBHW050538300426
44113CB00012B/2169